What Day Is It Today?

What day is it today?

It's Monday.

Monday

I read books
on Mondays.

What day is it today?

It's Tuesday.

Tuesday

I visit my grandma on Tuesdays.

What day is it today?

It's Wednesday.

Wednesday

I ride my bike
on Wednesdays.

What day is it today?

It's Thursday.

I play the guitar
on Thursdays.

What day is it today?

It's Friday.

Friday

I eat ice cream
on Fridays.

What day is it today?

It's Saturday.

Saturday

I make lunch
on Saturdays.

What day is it today?

It's Sunday.

Sunday

I watch movies
on Sundays.

Let's learn more about New Year's Day.

Color the firework.